THE FEELINGS KEEPER

NING SHIJIE'S REFLECTION SPEAKS TO HERE

JOHN J. A. MARTZHALL

Copyright © John J. A. Martzhall
All Rights Reserved.

This book has been published with all efforts taken to make the material error-free after the consent of the author. However, the author and the publisher do not assume and hereby disclaim any liability to any party for any loss, damage, or disruption caused by errors or omissions, whether such errors or omissions result from negligence, accident, or any other cause.

While every effort has been made to avoid any mistake or omission, this publication is being sold on the condition and understanding that neither the author nor the publishers or printers would be liable in any manner to any person by reason of any mistake or omission in this publication or for any action taken or omitted to be taken or advice rendered or accepted on the basis of this work. For any defect in printing or binding the publishers will be liable only to replace the defective copy by another copy of this work then available.

Goddess who takes the form of nine girls from the stars, with the title of queen empresses, these philosophical icons of self-coexistence, in the metaverse of the small blue world are 9 half-steps constituting 3 tritones between two musical notes of a tetrachord in the melodic pattern.

Contents

Preface

Ning Shijie manages to identify "The Feelings Keeper", as a character inhabiting the broad abstract field of the human mind, descending to the heart taking the form of innumerable feelings, Ning Shijie establishes the self-coexistence between her and the feelings manifested inside herself; "The Feelings Keeper" is the reaction materialized in unexpected circumstances in her life, this reaction is a source of energy used to create a new reality, Ning Shijie's cunning becomes the ability to understand inside herself "The feelings keeper" obtaining a benefit, thus, she manages to avoid being deceived by her own feelings, the cunning used with herself becomes a fundamental tool to achieve self-coexistence in her daily life; for Ning Shijie the silence of thoughts is attitude, it is understanding that through the senses "The feelings keeper" manifests inside herself, it is understanding the importance of dominating feelings because the circumstances around her manifest "The feelings keeper" inside her ; Ning Shijie dominates her own feelings of hers by managing to create the ideal reality in her lifestyle.Luo Jun Chang's obtains a code in the form of a pendant that he gives to Ning Shijie's, she manages to identify this code inside herself named "The Feelings Keeper", the code is a character inhabiting the broad abstract field of the human mind, descending to the heart taking the form of innumerable feelings, Ning Shijie establishes the self-coexistence between her and the feelings manifested inside herself; "The Feelings Keeper" is the reaction materialized in unexpected circumstances in her life, this reaction is a source of energy used to create a new reality, Ning Shijie's cunning becomes the ability to understand inside herself "The feelings keeper" obtaining a benefit, thus, she manages to avoid being deceived by her own feelings, the cunning used with herself becomes a fundamental tool to achieve self-coexistence in her daily life; for Ning Shijie the silence of thoughts is attitude, it is understanding that through the senses "The feelings keeper" manifests inside herself, it is understanding the importance of dominating feelings because the circumstances around her manifest "The feelings keeper" inside her ; Ning Shijie dominates her own feelings of hers by managing to create the ideal reality in her lifestyle.

Prologue

We are a reflection of many feelings; the feel is keeped with the thoughts that bloom in our minds like a pansy flower whose petals are "the feelings keepers" that descend to our hearts, reflecting fascinating colors being feelings materialized through a spontaneous reaction under unexpected circumstances; cunning with the silence of thoughts will persuade "the feelings keeper" in you and in people.

CHAPTER ONE

2:00 AM, the sound of the clock in Ning Shijie's room

2:00 AM, the sound of the clock in Ning Shijie's room wakes her up, the weight of her eyelids does not prevent she from observing the green pansy flower reflected in the large mirror of her room towards the left side of her bed; she sits and staring at her reflection in the mirror while perceives something unusual that does not baffle her.a. The reflection of Ning Shijie: I'm a reflection of yourself! I contemplate a brightness polaris in your sweet eyes, by perceive the cunning that silences the ideas of the mind while you breathe fresh air, achieving to hide that you are like me; I'm that reaction in unexpected circumstances, I'm "The feelings keeper".

6:00 AM, as if it were a simple breathe time passes quickly, Ning Shijie clears her gaze and without wonder she understands that she reflects everything she thinks and feels; That brief flicker in her gaze does not prevent Ning Shijie from continuing to observe the green pansy flower that reflects the mirror in her room.

b. Ning Shijie: With cunning, i dispersed thoughts like you dominating the imagination with the silence of thoughts, understanding in unexpected circumstances the reaction that quickly descends to my heart as something misleading that I'm not.

CHAPTER TWO

10:00 AM, Ning Shijie looks at her watch

10:00 AM, Ning Shijie looks at her watch, it's time to organize the luggage she will take for her trip; from the window of the house next door, Luo Jun Chang an extraordinarily recognized writerman, drinks coffee while contemplates Ning Shijie through the large window of her room; she notices Luo Jun Chang's attention looking him in the eyes while using a ribbon with both hands to hold the volume of her silky hair and continue preparing her journey; Ning Shijie has the ability to understand her daily life to avoid being deceived by the reaction generated under this unexpected circumstance; she is ready to leave her house and when she descends the stairs approaches the main door whose crystalline surface allows her to visualize the reflection of a red pansy flower.

a. *The reflection of Ning Shijie:* I'm a reflection of someone! That reaction, which is generated by your imagination when it transforms the infused thoughts in your mind by the personality or behavior of others, keeps the feelings and instincts as it quickly descends to your heart from your mind.

2:00 PM, Ning Shijie opened the front door and left her house securing the lock while holding her luggage to one side;

then she took several steps forward, but finally decided to look again at the door that once again reflected the red pansy flower on the outer surface of the door; refraining from involuntarily creating ideas and representations of reality in her mind, Ning Shijie avoided maintaining the reaction that would surely take hold of her by reflecting the same behavior of Luo Jun Chang.

b. *Ning Shijie:* My thoughts have been moderated by the silence of thoughts, blooming with dominion the reaction that keeps the feelings and instincts in the flower of the thought, whose petals descend quickly from my mind to my heart like sunlight on the earth at noon.

CHAPTER THREE

6:00 PM, at sunset

6:00 PM, at sunset, Ning Shijie begins to cross the lake park near the shore; she raises her right arm to look at the clock that announces a rapid passing of time without apparent explanation; Ning Shijie continues walking and directs her attention to the lake unexpectedly observing in the water the reflection of an orange pansy flower.

a. The reflection of Ning Shijie: I'm a reflection all the time! Day and night your mind without autonomy keeps the reaction under unexpected circumstances; it is "the feelings keeper" extending like water to your heart reflecting selectively through colors, moods and instincts that cannot be dominated in you.

10:00 PM, Night has come and while Ning Shijie takes a deep breath, she continues walking to cross a bridge in the center of the park that separates the two shores of the lake; over the bridge she contemplates in the water the moonlight that illuminates the night, without losing sight of the pansy flower reflected in the lake that unexpectedly turns the orange color of its petals into a white color announcing that the domain was granted to her through the silence of thoughts.

b. Ning Shijie: I contemplate in my heart to "the feelings keeper" day and night, being the petals of the pansy flower that by my will have been dominated by the silence of thoughts, while i breathe walking to where the sun is hiding.

CHAPTER FOUR

2:00 AM, near the bridge

2:00 AM, near the bridge on the other shore Ning Shijie arrives at the train station, she tackles the passenger car and takes a seat; being a professional of the fine arts of music, Ning Shijie will attend the conference that will be held in the city but no one has confirmed the exact information about the hotel where she will be staying; at that moment her phone with no signal held by her left hand perches on her leg after several attempts to communicate without any response, she breathes as she tilts the chair back to sleep. Time passes quickly, suddenly Ning Shijie opens her eyes and watches the window glass in front of her reflecting a white pansy flower.

a. The reflection of Ning Shijie: I'm a reflection of yourself! While you breathe i contemplate your heart perceiving the silence of thoughts in "the feelings keeper", like the white color in the petals of pansy flower willing to selectively reflect moods of your new reality.

6:00 AM, the train continues its way to the city; Ning Shijie goes to the food passenger car to enjoy a hot chocolate drink; Ning Shijie's attention is drawn outside the train by the crescent moon in the dark early morning sky; she blinks subtly watching again the white pansy flower reflected in the glass of the window.

b. *Ning Shijie:* From the sky, the brightness into the "black moon" is reflected, by the sweet taste of the only pleasant thought under unexpected circumstances, being petals white throbbing in my heart while i breathe silencing ideas in my mind.

CHAPTER FIVE

10:00 AM, upon arrival in the city

10:00 AM, upon arrival in the city, Ning Shijie receives a text message on her phone indicating the information regarding her accommodation and she goes to the train station exit; a friendly taxi driver whose priority is to take care of his two daughters, as a father he identifies with Ning Shijie and approaches her by offering her services to transfer her safely to the hotel, that instinct of protection seizes Ning Shijie and with absolute tranquility she cordially accepts; in front of the hotel, she leaves the vehicle thanking the taxi driver for bringing her; As the taxi drives away, before entering the hotel Ning Shijie observes on the bright surface of the revolving door the reflection of a pansy black moon.

a. The reflection of Ning Shijie: I'm a reflection of someone! In the hearts people's, ideas of their reality is perceived through "the feelings keeper" which reflects moods and instincts coming from memories modified by the imagination, persuading you to a common behavior.

2:00 PM, Ning Shijie crosses the door of the hotel and she is immediately attended by the manager who makes her record pleased to offer accommodation to a personality of international stature; suddenly, several people with infinite joy come to Ning Shijie in search of the opportunity to take a picture next to their great star and with their due approval Ning Shijie decides to share this same joy. After the unexpected welcome, go up to the elevator that stops on the ninth floor and while accommodating a beautiful pendant delivered to her by Luo Jun Chang and that is hanging around her neck, walks towards the hall; Ning Shijie stands in front of her bedroom door and for a moment observes the bright surface above the door reflecting a pansy black moon.

b. *Ning Shijie:* I have seen all colors of the pansy flower are moods and instincts reflected by "the feelings keeper" being "black moon" petals throbbing in my heart pigmented by my decision to selectively absorb, the ideas in people's reality.

6:00 PM, Ning Shijie enters the hotel room

6:00 PM, Ning Shijie enters the hotel room, she puts her luggage next to the bed and the phone on the table, it has been a long journey and time is running fast; when she sees the night approaching she begins to prepare the bedroom; at the table, her phone receives the news that will make her night something sublime; Through a text message sent by the music producer she works for, the first results of her most recent record work are made official; servers hired on the network reported that as of the launch date, 3.6 billion downloads of the musical composition have been made and continue to increase!. With her sleepwear, Ning Shijie takes her phone from the table and on the glass can not help observing the reflection of a black moon pansy flower whose center intensely reveals the flaming yellow iris perceived by Ning Shijie as the glory of the sun rising in the east.

a. *The reflection of Ning Shijie:* I'm a reflection all the time! Your mind without autonomy, has been day and night a pansy flower "black moon" whose iris of fire absorbs the ideas of reality reflecting all involuntary moods, in the black petals that quickly descends from your mind to your heart.

10:00 PM, a determinant smile on Ning Shijie's lips announces the series of simultaneous feelings that flow through her body from the feet to the head; the feeling of possessing everything, the feeling of enjoying with satisfaction, the feeling of absolute glory, the feeling of being loved, the feeling of being heard, the feeling of guiding, the feeling of ascending to heaven being present on earth, these are the feelings that take hold of her; adopting a mood determined by absolute happiness, Ning Shijie breathes as she closes her eyes for a moment to understand that glory has been bestowed upon her; when she opens her eyes again, she looks at the phone that once again reflects on the glass the black moon pansy flower, whose flaming iris expands intensifying the yellow color to the ends of the flower.

b. *Ning Shijie:* Like an instinctive sunrise of joy in summer, my feet move with the autonomy necessary to shake the reality while they pigment yellow the black petals throbbing in my heart day and night, seeing an impossible dream come true.

CHAPTER SEVEN

2:00 AM, Ning Shijie sleeps

2:00 AM, Ning Shijie sleeps, the luxurious surroundings of the room with the naked eye generates an indescribable harmony, the bed is very comfortable to the touch, the insulation inside prevents the entry of any sound, and the air offers a slight aroma of fresh essences that can be savored; with surprise but pleasantly Ning Shijie sees Luo Jun Chang for a moment in her dreams while subtly waking up perceiving the gentleness of her surrounding; when she gets up from the bed she turns on the light in the room to closely observe the large glass aquarium that suddenly reflects a black moon pansy flower, whose petals turn red from the ends of the flower.

a. The reflection of Ning Shijie: I'm a reflection of yourself! A new reality, is to understand that you cunningly perceive "the feelings keeper" as a blooming of spring in the light of your senses, through people, places or objects that inevitably infuse thoughts in your mind transformed into moods and instincts in your heart.

6:00 AM, Ning Shijie walks towards the bed while remembering her first meeting with Luo Jun Chang that as a good poet with beautiful and encouraging words he approached Ning Shijie at the entrance of her house that is a few steps from where he lives; the passage of time was determinant, Luo Jun Chang handed in the hands of Ning Shijie the beautiful pendant he made and with which both strengthened their friendship since through the pendant she understood how to use cunning along with the silence of thoughts, to have domain of "the feelings keeper" in herself and in people; Ning Shijie directs her gaze to the large glass aquarium that reflects a red pansy flower whose iris intensifies its flaming yellow color while the flower's petals simultaneously descend to Ning Shijie's heart as Luo Jun Chang's memories increase.

b. Ning Shijie: With my hands on my chest, I have contemplated scarlet petals throbbing in my heart; It is someone whom I am interested in continuing to frequent, because of my decision to selectively absorb that idea of reality, while dominating the feelings keeper cunningly.

CHAPTER EIGHT

10:00 AM Ning Shijie leaves the room

10:00 AM Ning Shijie leaves the room, crosses the corridor to go up to the elevator, goes down to the first floor and tackles a vehicle in front of the hotel that is waiting for her to transport her to the auditorium; upon arrival Ning Shijiese may notice that the screens located on the outskirts of the great hall have the attention of approximately two thousand three hundred people, whose purpose is to enter. With a security scheme provided for these occasions, Ning Shijie enters the auditorium that has exceeded the maximum quota; five thousand nine hundred people stand in front of Ning Shijie while clapping fervently; in the first row Luo Jun Chang contemplates the entrance of Ning Shijie to the stage; she looks him in the eyes and continues to take a seat with a personality and decisive behavior obtained by her experience of persuasion due to the use of the pendant. Ning Shijie directs her gaze to the audience in front of her and contemplates it as a huge crystal that reflects its equivalence in black moon pansy flowers whose petals at that moment turn violet from the ends, blooming in the minds of each of these people as a reflection of Ning Shijie.

a. The reflection of Ning Shijie: I'm a reflection of someone! You have persuaded to "the feelings keeper" in people's, using your senses and the silence of thoughts to reflect with the autonomy of your personality and behavior an original moods, based on the experience that infuse autumnal pansies in their minds.

2:00 PM, ending the conference, Ning Shijie raises her right arm by moving the palm of her hand to thank the people for attending while the entire audience shudders; Ning Shijie walks towards the exit with the satisfaction of doing her great work as a musical artista and before passing the door she turns to be observed once again throughout the auditorium; at that time, the reflection of Ning Shijie is seven thousand two hundred violet pansy flowers whose iris intensifies its flaming yellow color, while the petals of the flower descend simultaneously to the hearts of the people who yearn for the next encounter with their great star.

b. Ning Shijie: Violet petals throb in my heart as I breathe the fresh scent of a shared pansy whose color frequency has been transformed, being moods and instincts in the people's reflected by "the feelings keeper", when they achieve balance in their new reality.

CHAPTER NINE

6:00 PM, returning to the hotel

6:00 PM, returning to the hotel and without mishaps, begins the Ning Shijie itinerary that is scheduled for the next 18 months, making 72 presentations in different major cities of the 22 world regions. After leaving the hotel heading to the airport and boarding the plane, Ning Shijie is meditating while listening with her favorite headphones the latest musical notation arrangements in the melody of the composition; Ning Shijie observes through the window of the plane, that vastness of the ocean that suddenly reflects a colossal dark blue pansy flower.

a. *The reflection of Ning Shijie:* I'm a reflection all the time! I admire with fascination the cunning of your conscience when you use it to persuade me of reflect selectively in your heart or that of people's, the moods and instincts which intensify day and night as extraordinary melodies are heard accompanied by precious voices.

10:00 PM, what was once a dream, for Ning Shijie has now become the absolute reality, hearing that welcome melody that emits the voice coming from billions of pansy flowers reflecting the most precious feelings when they keep the music of thought that descends to all their hearts. Ning Shijie slides her headphones looking back to the window pane inside the plane whose reflection is a blue pansy flower.

b. *Ning Shijie:* I would like to hear again the sound of the most precious pansies transformed into feelings, being our voices accompanied by melodies in short days, long nights and low temperatures, like a dream of blue petals throbbing in all hearts.

The Firstself-coexistence Metaverse On Web 3

The abstract field of the mind, is the connection between the metaverse of the small blue world and the people who identify themselves as philosophical icons of self-coexistence; in this metaverse the thoughts of each people's involuntarily create reality using feelings, "The feelings keeper" is an abstract character in the hearts of people, this character use thoughts to created the reality, in the small blue world, lear to coexist with "the feelings keeper" inside eachone is to empower any lifestyle.